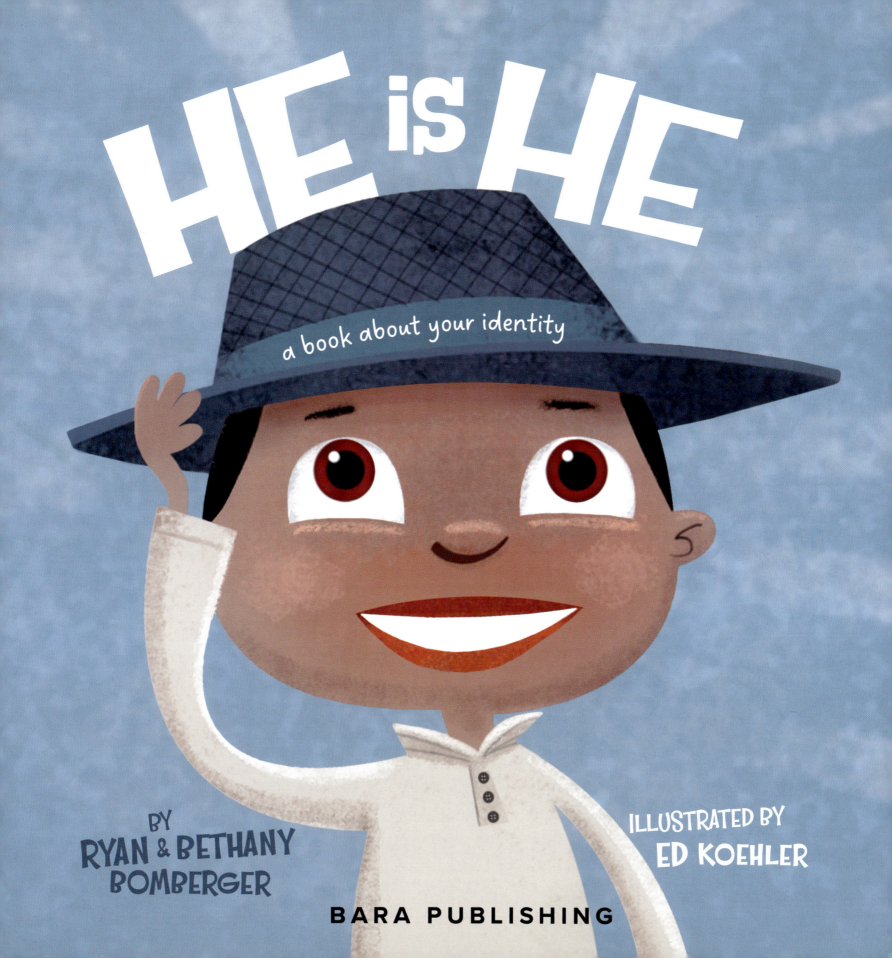

B
BARA
PUBLISHING

Published in the U.S.A. by Bara Publishing
BaraPublishing.com
For inquiries: info@barapublishing.com

© 2023 by Ryan & Bethany Bomberger

Book editing, design and layout by Ryan Scott Bomberger

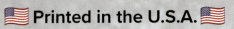 **Printed in the U.S.A.**
Signature Book Printing
sbpbooks.com

ISBN: 978-0-9972036-4-6
Library of Congress Control Number: 2023920202

Although we want you to share this wonderful book with everyone you know, we highly recommend gifting it, not copying it. Of course, if you want to promote how much you love the book on social media, feel free to post the (unaltered) cover or favorite image in the book! Here comes the legal stuff. No part of this publication may be reproduced, distributed or transmitted in any form or by any means, including photocopying, recording, or other electronic or mechanical methods (well except for the whole **tell-your-friends-and-family-online** caveat), without the prior written permission of the copyright owners and publisher of the book. None of the characters in this book may be used or reproduced for any other purposes.

DEDICATION

To all the Godly men in our lives – *dads, brothers, grandpas, uncles, pastors, friends and mentors* – thank you for loving and shaping us into who we are today.

Boys will be boys! Why? Because they're exactly who God designed them to be: loving, strong, protective, curious, brave, kind, creative and adventurous.

To every boy who reads this book... be who God meant you to be!

—Ryan & Bethany Bomberger

He is he.

He *is* not she.

not we.

He is he.

He's a son.

He's a brother.

He's a father.

He's a Grampy.

He is he.

He's a mentor.

He's a world

changing inventor.

He's a pastor.

He's a coura

geous life-saver.

he is free

to be who God meant him to be.

THe

What does the Bible say?

The Bible has **a lot** to say about how and why God created us. God designs everything with a purpose. Boys and girls are the same in some ways and *very* different in others. This makes life *wonderful!* Here are a few verses that can remind you how **special** you are.

1. "So God created mankind in His own image, in the image of God He created them; male and female he created them." **Genesis 1:27 (NLT)**

2. "For You made the parts inside me. You put me together inside my mother." **Psalms 139:13 (NLV)**

3. "For we are God's masterpiece. He has created us anew in Christ Jesus, so we can do the good things he planned for us long ago." **Eph 2:10 (NLT)**

4. "Be watchful, stand firm in the faith, act like men, be strong. Let all that you do be done in love." **1 Corinthians 16:13-14 (ESV)**

5. "For this is how God loved the world: He gave His one and only Son, so that everyone who believes in Him will not perish but have eternal life." **John 3:16 (NLT)**

What does science say?

God created the Laws of Nature, which means He created science. Science repeatedly proves Biblical truths correct over and over again. Here are some scientific facts about how boys and girls are different in important ways. And we know it all starts **waaaaaay** before we're born!

1. As soon as we exist, something special inside each of us (called DNA) makes a person either a boy or a girl. That DNA never changes, no matter *how* we feel.

2. Doctors know *long* before we're born whether we are males or females. They use a special machine to see inside a mother's womb. The image is called an *ultrasound*.

3. There are *thousands* of physical differences between boys and girls. Some pretend this isn't so. Boys' brains, faces, hearts, lungs, and other body parts are different than girls'.

4. From football to swimming to soccer and volleyball, it's important to have separate boys' & girls' sports teams to give us *all* a chance to *shine*. It's fun to compete when it's fair.

5. Only females can get pregnant, carry babies inside of them and give birth. How amazing! No guy can ever do that. Even so, dads and moms are equal in value.

Get more info and resources at **www.HeisHe.org**

the authors

Bethany and Ryan Bomberger are the parents of four amazing kids: two girls and two boys. They are also the founders of The Radiance Foundation which is a faith-based, educational, 501c3 nonprofit. Their reach is global as they powerfully illuminate that every human life has God-given purpose. Their innovative and bold work has earned them massive mainstream media coverage including the NY Times, MSNBC, Fox News, CNN, The Christian Post, ABC News, NewsMax, Breitbart, NPR, Epoch Times, World, Washington Times, Washington Post and more.

Bethany Bomberger is an educator by profession. She taught for over a decade in public and private schools in both suburban and urban settings. As a homeschooling mama, she's an advocate for school choice. Bethany is the Executive Director of Radiance Foundation. She's an international public speaker, podcaster and author of several ground-breaking children's books including **HE IS HE**, **SHE IS SHE**, and **PRO-LIFE KIDS!**. From conferences to pregnancy center galas to Supreme Court rallies, she loves speaking about how Christ makes us stronger than our circumstances.

Ryan Bomberger is the Chief Creative Officer of The Radiance Foundation. He's an international public speaker, columnist, factivist, and author of **Not Equal: Civil Rights Gone Wrong, He Is He,** and **She Is She**. He has a passionate perspective on purpose. He was adopted and loved in a diverse family of fifteen (ten were adopted). Today, he's an Emmy Award-winning creative professional who designs messaging that's fearless, factual and freeing. Ryan keynotes at major conferences, pregnancy center galas, middle & high schools, colleges (including Harvard, Princeton, Columbia Law School, Penn State, Cornerstone University, Eureka College, Quinnipiac, Georgia Tech), churches and more.

Bethany and Ryan met and fell in love at Regent University where they earned their master's degrees. They are the blessed parents of both biological and adopted kiddos: Rai Rai, Kai, Aliyah & Justice. The Bombergers are passionately building a culture that values life, planned or unplanned.

Visit us at www.radiance.life

the illustrator

Ed Koehler is a freelance illustrator specializing in fun, lively art for children's books, educational materials, and any variety of print and online products. His work has been published around the world, and he's received numerous awards from the Evangelical Press Association and Associated Church Press. He's a member of the Society of Children's Book Writers and Illustrators as well as the St. Louis Artists Guild. Working with publishers, designers, and product developers throughout the world, Ed creates fun art for books, curriculum, magazines, packaging and all kinds of kid-friendly products.

People around the globe have been entertained and inspired by Ed's whimsical style. Bethany and Ryan first worked with Ed to create the history-making **Pro-Life Kids!** book. Together, the Bombergers and Koehler have created more life-affirming books such as **She is She** and **He is He.** They want to shift culture through creativity, truth & love.

MEET HENRY BOMBERGER, JR.

This book is dedicated to a man of God who was a loving husband to my amazing mom (Andrea Bomberger) and devoted father to thirteen. Yes, thirteen children! Ten of us were adopted. He treated us all the same, which means he loved us a whole lot! He and mom showed us we were all meant to be, planned or "unplanned".

My dad loved to laugh. He loved to play. He loved to take photos and capture funny and special moments at the beach, at parks, or just at home. He worked hard and owned a big family store in Lancaster County, PA, called Bombergers Store. He was super generous and always tried to help others in need even though times were often hard raising a family of fifteen. One of his favorite Bible verses was Philippians 4:4 – *"Rejoice in the Lord always, and again I say, rejoice."*

The dad I loved passed away on January 22, 2021. It hurt my heart so much, but he gave me the greatest gifts I could ever have: being his son and knowing my Savior Jesus Christ. He made the world a much kinder, hopeful and joyful place.

—Ryan Bomberger (Henry's first adopted son)

Learn more about Henry Bomberger and his passion for adoption:

When your identity is rooted in ❊Christ❊ it won't be uprooted by everything else.

—Ryan & Bethany Bomberger